The Effects & Benefits of Music

"The right molding of ingenuous civil conduct lies in a well-grounded music education."

— *Lucius Plutarch,*
Greek biographer 46-AD 120

The Effects & Benefits of Music

Health, Emotion, Mind and Intellect in View

Frank Godwin Igboke

EXCELLER BOOKS®
A GLOBAL PRESS

ISBN: 978-81-19524-98-3

First published in India in 2024 by Exceller Books,
An imprint of GE Group
Address: G1, Dream Apartment, Degree College Road, Belgharia,
Kolkata, 700056, India
www.excellerbooks.com

Dedication

To my late Parent, Mrs. Paulina Ehbi Igboke1952 – 2015, and Mathew Igboke 1944 -2021, for nurturing me and instilling in me a love for music. Your influence has shaped my musical journey and this book is a testament to your legacy.

To Dapo Zion Kalejaiye 1969 -1999 and El Gideon Mathew Igboke 1978-1999, you may be gone to eternal rest, but the world still feels your impact through those of us you brought up and mentored musically and otherwise.

If you both had not ventured into music, I wouldn't have been in it today.

Rest in peace, all of you.

To my lovely family, siblings, older and younger, I love you all.

Acknowledgement

My beautiful and lovely wife, Mrs. Chioma Charity Frank Igboke, is a true gift from God. You are a blessing in my life. I thank God for giving me the inspiration, understanding, and ability to research and write the contents of this book. With God, nothing is impossible.
Glory be to God

Foreword

This book is a comprehensive exploration of the effects of music on humans in all its forms. It delves into the history of music, explores different genres, and explains the intricate reactions of the human brain to musical stimulation. By the end, you will feel more informed and knowledgeable about the profound impact of music on our lives.

The author takes us step by step through a well-researched and often startling revelation of music's strength, beauty, possibilities, and impact. Each chapter focuses on a different aspect, from basic listening pleasure to therapeutic, emotional, medical, and spiritual values of the power of music.

It is impossible to perceive music in the same light after reading this book. I strongly recommend this book to every parent, teacher, and artist individual. The nugget of knowledge contained here will open your mind to the power and possibilities music provides. You are guaranteed to view and approach music hereafter in a more purposeful, informed and appreciative manner.

Sonye Allana
Etiquette/Image Consult,
Public Speaking Expert, Blogger

Introduction

This book was inspired by the universal appeal of music, a gift from God to nature that transcends race, class, culture, and religion. It is a force that should be universally appreciated and accepted by humanity.

It all began when I was working as a music teacher in a school where music was made compulsory as part of the subject. However, a group of parents had reservations based on religious sentiment. This challenge led the head teacher and me to find a way to communicate the transformative power of music education. We believed that music, as a compulsory subject, could inspire and enlighten our pupils, regardless of their background or beliefs.

First, I needed to know whose idea it was that music should be taught in schools and why music should be part of the subject in school. My head teacher then handed me a copy of a curriculum, so I decided to research how the idea of music being taught in school began. Then, I discovered that the ancient Greeks had devised the idea. At one time in history, the Greeks significantly influenced Western civilization, so most European countries emulated every one of their activities. The discoveries I made are what this book contains, and this fact on the effects and benefits of music on our health, emotion, mind, and intellect are based on sciences and nature. Thanks for purchasing a copy of this book; I hope the knowledge provided in this book will expose you to a new perspective on music.

Yours truly,
Igboke Frank Godwin

Contents

We are so familiar with music that we often overlook its effects and benefits.

Chapter I
Music and How It Connects to You

Music is ubiquitous, heard daily in countless places—on the radio, television, and mobile phones, in places of worship, at social gatherings, in cars, during TV games, in toys, and even in advertisements on the streets and in markets.

Music refers to an organized sound that comprises of melody, rhythm, harmony and qualities such as pitch, duration, intensity, timbre and tempo and is generally grouped into three major styles, traditional or folk, orchestra or classical and popular or pop genres.

Traditional or folk refers to the style of music that is connected with particular people and their way of life. Classical refers to an organized style of music that requires much thinking to compose and perform. The style of music emerged in the Middle Ages European society around 1750, and it's still very much appreciated and accepted globally. Popular or pop refers to the style of music whose rhythm is appealing to a wider audience, mostly youth in urban development. Pop started from the early nineteen fifties till date.

Irrespective of the styles, the uses of music from the onset are versatile, most especially in contemporary times; music is used in social events, traditional purposes, in the media, in theatres, in movies, political rallies, in medical science and most especially for religious rituals. Aside from all the aspects listed above, music has other uses and benefits that most of us would never have imagined or know very little about. Some of you may already know but may not really be to the extent of how it is expatiated in this book. For better knowledge, let's look into the actual meaning or definition of what music is.

Music as It Is Defined

Although various intellectuals have different ways in which they define music based on their understanding, in all of the definitions, sound is mentioned as the main source or the ingredient by which music exists and without which music cannot exist, for example, a voice, an object in vibration or a string stretched from a point to another that is plucked. Sounds are generally produced as a result of waves in vibration, which are received in our ears and are sent to the brain through nerve fibres, where it is interpreted as tone or speech. In simple words, music is actually a type of sound that has been arranged in a way that pleases the ears. The sound referred to as music is different from all other sounds because it contains certain qualities that are not in other sounds that are heard. Our brains receive and process music differently because of its special features and characteristics.

Origin of Music

Various intellectuals have various notions about the origin of music. Some are based on religion, others on evolution, and also on archaeological facts. The use of sounds to communicate or arrange in a manner that pleases the ears to entertain, pass information, or express feelings began when primitive man developed the sense of organising sounds to make meaning to his or her ears.

It is purported that the primitive man may have been inspired by sounds that are heard when gathering dry bones or wood and also sounds made by birds and other animals, which he later derived a way of organising to excite his or her ears, thereby originating music. The religious belief about the origin of music is in accordance with the teachings from the holy men through the holy books such as the Bible, the Torah, the Quran, and the Hindu Vedas etc.

The Adjective Music

We cannot establish any fact that the primitive or the early men whose sounds from bones and dry woods may have inspired them to invent music actually had a name given to the art of arranging sounds in a way that pleases the ears as an adjective to describe it generally, but the fact remains that music started when men start to develop the sense of rhythm, and it was mainly a tribal affair in the beginning. According to history, the earliest known civilisations that used music extensively were the Sumerians, Egyptians, and Crete, then the Babylonians, Medes and Persians, the Hebrews, the Romans, and the Greeks, who later became a major influence on Western civilisation. Various folks might have a name that they refer to as art in their various cultures, but the Greeks were the first to refer to it as Mousike, which is translated as music in the English language. The literal meaning of the word mouse is the art of the muses; muses in Greek mythology refer to nine goddesses of art and sciences, which are believed to be in charge of invention, innovation, creativity and emotion. The Greeks, I believe, choose to use the adjective 'Mousike' to describe the art because of its intellectual and emotional connectivity to human entirety; the ancient Greeks made use of music to its fullest, and special places were built across Greek city-states called the orchestra, where public music performances take place, music was included as part of lessons taught in schools and musical schools were established independently.

Music and Humanity

The entirety of our existence as alive and active humans is centred on three things: the brain, the mind, and emotion. The brain is the organ inside the head that controls movement, thought, memory, and feelings. It is divided into the right and left cerebral hemispheres. The mind is the part of a person that makes them able to be aware of things, think, feel, and act based on what the brain sends.

Emotion is a strong feeling such as love, fear, or anger; it is the part of a person's character that consists of feelings generally.

Music is the only thing that connects with all three in special ways. It greatly influences and helps these aspects of humans function excellently and eliminates some chances of malfunctioning.

Music to Our Entirety

When a person listens to music, inside the ears are over four thousand nerve fibres which communicate the music directly to the brain, where it is specially processed, interpreted and distributed to our entire system, thereby influencing our thoughts, feelings and body actions, which explains the reason some people listen to music and tears roll down their eyes, others develop goose bumps, others fall in love by a mere hearing particular song, some people have special cases that when listening to soothing music the connection of the music with their brains causes what is called Piloerection. This reflex causes tiny muscles near our hair follicles to contract and raise the hair on our body.

The common physical response to music is that of the body, which includes certain gestures such as tapping of foot or hand to the rhythm, moving the head to the beat and the body stylishly in response; this justifies the purported claim that music can influence our actions. People who experience goosebumps when listening to soothing music have more fibres connecting their auditory cortex to the area of the brain responsible for emotion processing, although the case is rare.

An individual once told me that whenever she gets confused, all she does is listen to soothing music, which in turn restores her concentration and also enhances her performance. In 1999, I visited a clergy, and while talking, he said to me that we musicians have certain privileges clergies do not; he went further to say that there are cases when conducting exorcisms, music serves as a tool in addition to compelling demons out from the victims, but he categorically said it's only music with greater spiritual powers that has the ability to accomplish such purpose.

I was curious and needed to understand what he meant by music with greater spiritual powers.

Music with a very strong rhythm usually stimulates the brain to release a substance called adrenaline. Adrenaline is produced in the body when a person is excited. This causes the heart to beat faster and increases one's energy and ability to move quickly. As a result, your brain becomes more alert, and your blood sugar level rises to give you more energy at the time.

Music with Greater Spiritual Power

The universe is governed by powers that cannot be explained by mere human knowledge because we all depend on them. Forces beyond the physical carry out activities in favour of or against us. Humans consult with the supernatural, either through religion or other beliefs.

Music with greater spiritual powers refers to music that is connected with a realm higher than the natural, either based on religion or other forces. This means music can also be used to achieve spiritual objectives. Lots of music is connected to powers beyond the physical, positive or negative, so your choice of music should be made with discretion and based on your target.

Music is a powerful phenomenon which does more than just entertainment.

Chapter 2
The Effect of Music on Your Brain

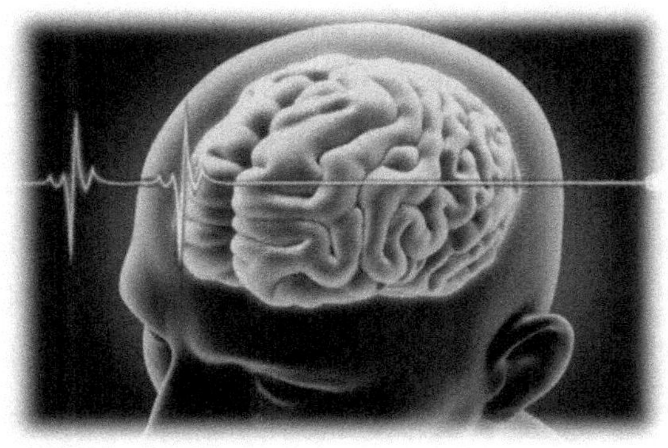

The organ inside the head that controls movements, thoughts, memories, and feelings is referred to as the brain; music is a powerful propeller which affects the brain by helping it to function at its best capacity, but how true is this claim? To prove this claim, there is first the need to know a bit about the brain and its structure. The cerebrum is the largest area of the brain and is divided into two parts called the left and the right hemispheres. The right hemisphere controls the left side of the body and is responsible for artistic expression; for example, the ability to draw, paint, and work with colours; that natural skill in you even to dress to match, to design, to arrange or as a lady to make up etc.

The right hemisphere is also responsible for understanding relationships in space, i.e. anything related to the Earth's atmosphere, weather, land, climate change, etc. The left hemisphere controls the right side of the body and is responsible for mathematical ability, problem-solving, language and decision-making. The brain controls how we take in, store, remember, and use information and responds to touch, taste and smell. Neuron sciences research has proven music to have a great influence on our brains because it is a stimulus to the brain.

A stimulus, in a simple term, refers to something that helps something develop better or more quickly. Music has been found to help the brain develop and function better because it is usually processed in the brain through receptors that sense and react to it. As a result, music influences the neural connections, thereby affecting other connectors that carry information to the other parts of the body, which in turn reflects in our actions.

When listening to soothing music, the nerves that deal with the auditory system in the brain are activated, especially in order for music to be heard; this process contributes to improving the brain in several ways. Music also enormously influences our intellectual abilities; the art of singing and playing musical instruments enhances brain functions by provoking the formation of certain chemicals called dopamine to be released, which causes a burst in our reasoning and ability to think in a coherent way and understand things, especially at an advance level.

Music Advantage

Most of the world's renowned scientists, inventors, philosophers, and influential leaders in history have one thing in common: They are all musically inclined or ardent lovers of music, which gives them an added advantage in their intellectual abilities and greatly affects their creativity.

For example, Pythagoras, a Greek philosopher considered to be the first true mathematician who proved the Pythagorean Theorem, was known to experiment with musical scales in most of his research, meaning he had musical abilities. Lucious Plutarch, a Greek biographer and the author of *Parallel Lives* believed the right moulding of ingenuous civil conduct lies in a well-grounded musical education, which means he was also musically inclined.

Albert Einstein, a world-renowned physicist, said, and I quote," I often think in music. I live my daydreams through music. I see my life in terms of music. Mr. Albert plays the violin very well.

Thomas Edison was a great lover of music. He was an ardent listener to classical music. History has it that when someone plays the piano, Mr. Edison would lean in close to the piano, listening to the melodies while experimenting with his inventions. The piano helped Edison experience the vibration in his skull.

According to neuron science, vibrations in the skull help enhance concentration and creativity. Mr Edison invented the phonograph, the first machine to record and playback. Based on this, part of what made these men successful and creative in their careers was their musical abilities.

There is always a great distinction between professionals with musical abilities and those without. The levels of creativity in people with musical skills are usually unique compared to those without the ability; this claim is justified by research conducted through brain scans on individuals with musical abilities and those without. The brain scans of people with musical skills show areas responsible for motor control, auditory processing, and spatial coordination to be quiet larger than those without the ability. People who can play musical instruments or sing songs excel in the following.

Language Development

The interconnectivity that links the two halves of the brain as a result of musical activity usually leads to more efficiency in information processing because the brain must concentrate on comprehending multiple stimuli. This helps a person understand phonemes and phonetics, including the logic to quickly pronounce words with the right accent to make meaning.

Spatial Intelligence

When involved in musical activity, the action potentials in the brain's two cerebral hemispheres are activated by empowering the interconnection between the two halves to become twice as powerful. This improves a person's ability to recognise shapes, angles, colours, and how things work technically. This skill is important in careers such as architecture, engineering, mathematicians, computer science, fine art, and surgeons.

Intelligent Quotient

The level of a person's ability to learn fast, understand how things work, and think logically to come up with solutions is referred to as intelligence. A quotient is a number obtained by dividing a number by another, which is used to rate a person's intelligence.

Musical skills help develop and increase one's creativity and ability to reason and quickly come up with solutions. Persons with musical ability learn fast, understand quickly, and retain information longer, except if they choose not to. According to psychologists, there are four types of quotients: intelligence, emotional, adversity and social. Intelligence refers to our ability to grasp, understand, memorise, retain, recall and solve problems.

The emotional quotient refers to one's ability to create and maintain a peaceful coexistence, manage time effectively, and be honest, respectful, and responsible.

A social quotient is an individual's ability to be organised, stress-free, and maintain a network of friends and businesses.

Your adversity quotient is your ability to endure tough situations without losing your mind. An individual with musical abilities has a ninety-nine per cent higher chance of surviving heartbreak than those without.

Music is connected to the entire quotient and has the ability to increase and improve it. Dr Agnes Chan conducted verbal and visual memory tests on ninety (90) students in the Chinese universe of Hong Kong and found that music stimulates the left side of the brain, thereby improving its overall functions and causing the entire brain to do better at other tasks.

Students aged 6 and 15 where involved in the experiment, those with musical abilities could recall significantly more words than those with no musical abilities, the research further shows that the longer we engage in musical lessons the better our verbal learning performances becomes.

Dr. A Chan study proves persons with musical skills learns and assimilates easily and can retain what they have been taught for as long as they need it.

Pupils who participate in musical lessons in or outside the school are far more intelligent than those who are not involved in musical lessons. Parent or guardians who deny their children from participating in musical activities are simply limiting their chances of becoming more intellectually sound. Participating in musical lessons does not necessarily mean the person is going to become a musician, but because of its benefits to our health, emotion and intellect, including spirituality.

Some of you might have read or heard about Dr Benjamin Carson (The Magic Finger), a renowned paediatrician neurosurgeon, a very successful medical doctor; I can argue that a certain percentage of his success is based on the fact that he is an ardent lover of classical music and possesses musical abilities because on his interview the first day at John Hopkins hospital he made reference to a classical piece composed by George Frederick Handel in 1742, titled MESSIAH.

Ben Carson, as a teenager, loved listening to classical music and preferred it to pop, which predominates and was widely enjoyed by his contemporaries at the time. In his reference to Handel's music, he said, and I quote. "I believe we are all capable of doing miracles; look at Handel, how can he compose something like Messiah in only three weeks." when you listen to that classical piece by George Frederick Handel, an orchestra musician who existed in the 16th century, whose music is still very much appreciated and impactful till date, you will indeed understand why Dr Carson made reference to it. When asked if he loves classical music? Dr. Carson replied with emphasis and said I love it. His love for classical music and his musical abilities help a great deal in increasing his intelligence quotient and spatial intelligence, enabling him to understand the logic behind the technicalities in surgery and in other aspects of medical science. Aside from that, he is naturally talented.

Music enlarges the brain's ability to process information, which is beneficial in areas such as behaviour, skill development, the ability to successfully mix with different groups of people, and coordination in general.

*Our reasoning and behavior may sometimes be influenced
by the music we frequently listen to.*

Chapter 3

Health Benefits of Music

Music has been proven to have the ability to repair damage in our brains and restore lost memories. According to research, when involved in musical activities such as singing, playing musical instruments, or sight-reading, music scores trigger more neural connections, which usually amount to certain positive responses. This, in turn, helps to improve the condition of persons suffering from brain-related ailments.

Alzheimer's is a common health challenge mostly with elderly people; a person suffering from Alzheimer's at an advanced level usually loses the ability to interact with others and eventually stops speaking completely, but when

30

listening to familiar music, such an individual often visibly lightens up and attempt to sing along, when this is done often his or her memories begins to recall the activities that took place on the first day of he or she first heard the music.

In the case of chronic stress, the individual quickly regains as he or she listens to soothing music, which automatically reduces the stress by lowering the stress hormones Croatia.

Listening to mild, calm and soothing music eliminates nervousness by quickly relaxing certain brain nerves to stabilise the mind. Music is also very effective in improving persons with autism.

Autism is a mental condition in which a person finds it difficult to communicate or form relationships with others due to the inability of certain brain cells to function as they ought to.

A person with autism gradually improves when he or she is involved in musical activities such as singing and learning to play a musical instrument, most especially the piano or the drum kits. The improvement comes as a result of music as a stimulant to the brain, so by engaging the person in musical activities, the area responsible for action potentials becomes reactivated, and the person starts to communicate and develop relationships with others gradually.

The Effect of Music on Down Syndrome

Down syndrome is a condition in which mostly a child does not respond to normal activity as he or she ought to have at his or her age due to certain brain dysfunctions. The ailment is usually associated with a very low intelligence quotient (IQ), and as a result, the child or person becomes very slow in learning and unable to act smart compared to his or her contemporaries. The condition is so because there are no proper interactions within the neurons in the brain and those responsible for sending information to another part of the body that would have enabled the child or person to act intelligently.

A person with Down syndrome improves when he or she becomes involved in musical activities. Engaging an autistic person in listening to music helps greatly improve his or her condition because a burst of music can propel gestures such as tapping the foot, nodding the head, or tapping fingers in response to the rhythm. Parents or guardians having children or relatives with Down syndrome should employ the services of a music therapist or specialist alongside side with any medications as recommended by the medics. A calm and suiting rhythm helps to relax the nerves, and music with a very strong rhythm gives certain body responses. The same music should be played repeatedly to their hearing until their mind assimilates it.

The Effect of Music on Seizure Disorder

Seizure disorder, commonly known as epilepsy, is a condition which causes convulsions in an individual and is usually accompanied by impaired consciousness. This occurs when there is an interruption of the normal connection between nerve cells as a result of uncontrolled electric disturbances in the brain. Brain seizure is usually triggered by tension and excess noise or emotional disturbances. Music helps a great deal to improve the condition as listening to suiting music synchronises the brain by stopping any interruption between the nerves, which automatically helps to stabilise the condition, but only very calming and soothing music does that.

The Effect of Music on Speech Impediment

A defect in a person's inability to speak, such as a lisp or stammer, for example, is referred to as a speech impediment or impairment. I watched a performance by a nineteen-year-old girl, Amanda Mammana. She was called up for her presentation on America's Got Talent in December 2022; she came up stage and began to stutter as she said these words,

"I have a bit of a speech impediment, and it is definitely something that causes me to shy away and hide, but I don't stutter when I sing".

When a person engages in singing, it directly stimulates the muscles involved in speech production. These include the mouth and tongue muscles, respiration, phonation, articulation, and resonance. Singing makes speech processing possible because it uses the same area of the brain that involves communication. Engaging a person with speech impairment in singing will help correct that aspect of the brain responsible for producing speech processing.

The Effect of Music on Hypertension

Hypertension is a health condition that occurs when the blood pressure is higher than normal due to emotional stress as a result of anxiety in most cases. When a hypertensive person listens to calm and very suiting music, the hormones Croatia responsible for stress are lowered to ease tension and relax nerves.

The Effect of Music on Depression

Depression refers to that mental condition in which an individual feels very sad to the point of being unable to carry out his or her normal activities and, in some cases, loses appetite. Depression is common, especially in youth, due to heartbreaks, disappointment, etc. Music is very effective in helping persons with depression regain themselves. By listening to familiar, mild and soothing music, the person quickly becomes conscious of his or her mind that is lost at a time and then begins to feel at ease.

The Effect of Music on Amnesia

Amnesia is a mental condition in which an individual loses his or her memories partially or completely. The condition is so because the area responsible for processing and retaining information in the brain ceases to function properly. When such an individual is made to often listen to familiar music, the nerves responsible for receiving, processing and retaining information in the brain will become strengthened and reactivated, so the person starts recalling events and circumstances that occurred at the time when he or she heard the music in the past.

The advantage of exposing children to music is that they become familiar with it later, which is like saving for a rainy day. If a child who is now an adult develops any brain-related ailment that likely causes memory loss, that particular music the person is familiar with, especially during his or her childhood, can be the very point of helping him or her recall his or her memory.

The Effect of Music on Insomnia

Insomnia is a health condition in which a person loses sleep at night, but Listening to soft and appealing music when it is time to sleep helps to relax the nerves for the individual to fall asleep easily. In 1990, a theory known as the Mozart effect was popularised. The theory suggests that listening to music composed by Wolfgang Amadeus Mozart, a classical musician who existed in the seventeenth century, can help improve the conditions of persons with brain disorders. The reason is that music composed by Mozart usually has a beat-per-minute pattern that is repeated throughout; continual listening to his music can help improve an individual with any brain-related ailment and also causes a burst in the increase of his or her intelligence quotients. Soft and mild music that is heard at a moderate volume is more effective in improving health conditions, as outlined before now. Normal hearing is between 40 and 45 decibels; hearing exceeding 80 and 85 decibels damages the ear. Music should always be played on a moderate level, not exceeding 45 decibels or less, for effective sensitivity.

When it comes to suiting music, everyone has his or her preferred genres and styles. Suiting music to Mr A might be classical, but to Mr B, it might be traditional folk; to another person, it might be pop. Endeavour to know the style of music that suits you and always enjoy its rhythm on a moderate volume. According to stress management principles and practice, when singing, our entire body resounds and vibrates to a certain point; these gentle vibrations help tissues relax and dilate or swell, which possibly can radiate or suppress physical pains to some percentages.

The principles further suggest that listening to suitable music may also reduce anxiety in pregnant women and promote relaxation during labour and delivery.

Calm and soothing music is like medicine to the mind, healing emotional maladies.

Chapter 4
How Music Influences Our Actions

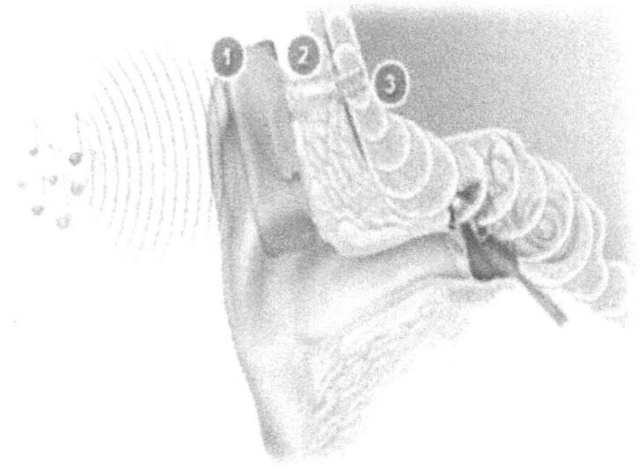

The kind of music we love and often listen to influences our thinking and is reflected in our actions or behaviour. Naturally, we humans react based on what is heard; we become aggressive when we hear offensive words and calm down when we are softly spoken to; words can destabilise and bring relief. Music is, in a way is, a language on its own that communicates to our spirit and soul. Music is also like the food we eat; nutritionists have proved that a person is what he or she eats; when you eat healthy, you will also look healthy, so also it is with music; we are a reflection of the kind of music we love to listen to. Music affects our mood, concentration, creativity and ability to learn and act because, as a stimulus, when processed by the brain, it, in turn, propels reactions that reflect in our actions.

The processing of music as a stimulus in the brain influences the neural connections within the brain which also affects other neurons connectors that carry information from the brain to the rest part of the body, this justifies and established the fact that the kind of music we often love to listen reflect in the way we think and in turn act.

Influence of Music on Our Body

The common response when listening to music is dance, but the body's response to music goes beyond just dancing. An experiment was conducted at Iowa State University, Texas Department of Human Services USA; some five hundred (500) high school students were involved. The students were divided into two groups and kept in separate places, and a piece of music with a very strong rhythm was played to the first group and, at the same time, soft and mild music to the other group; after some time, the two groups were taking to a special laboratory where their tensions were checked, the group that listened to the music with very strong rhythm and tempo where discovered to have very high tension, why the other group was the opposite.

To actually establish the fact, the experiment was repeated vice vassal, and the result was still the same; with that, the researchers were able to establish the fact that the type of music a person listens to affects his or her actions at a time or generally. A person who always listens to aggressive music might start behaving in such a manner with time. A person who loves to listen to lousy and non-sense-making music will also act in that line, and a person who loves to listen to music that expresses love will also think and act in that direction.

Our actions and reactions are based on what the mind is fed with continually; the type of music we are listening to at a time will influence whatever activity we are involved in at the time; here are some examples,

Influence of Music While Driving

Listening to music while driving helps the mind to concentrate better and the person driving to have excellent control because, at that point, every part of the brain is activated to function accurately and competent as a result of the music he or she is listening to and also helps to lower stress hormones to enable the person to drive and cover much distance without being weary. However, it is important to note that the rhythm and tempo of music that is heard while driving have tendencies to affect the way a person drives at the time. Individuals who have a woofer installed in their cars and usually play music with a very strong rhythm usually drive hasty in a way but have excellent control to manoeuvre in case of port holes or eventuality. Those who love to listen to soft and mild music while driving tend to drive cautiously and smoothly and have excellent control to manoeuvre in case of any eventuality.

Influence of Music While Drawing

An artist who draws or paints does best when appropriate music is played in the background. Aside from inspiring an artist's creativity, music fully activates the area of the brain responsible for all body movement and coordination (motor) and the ability to understand the shapes and blend colours to make sense (spatial intelligence), which helps the artist create a masterpiece.

Music also relaxes the mind; for those in the profession of painting, music is of great advantage; listening to a piece of soothing music as an artist while painting helps you to concentrate better and also triggers your creativity. History has records of great and renowned painters whose works are very much appreciated to date. Example: a Russian abstract painter by the name Wassily Kandinsky, his works were deeply inspired by music; we also have painters like Leonardo, Giorgione, Tintoretto, Jean Auguste Dominique Ingres, and Eugene Delacroix who were also excellent musicians and their creative work in the field of painting was inevitably awesome.

Influence of Music on Labor Activity

The progress that is recorded or achieved in manual labour, along with singing or music played in the background, is always quick, better, and excellent compared to labour with no music accompanied. This is because the rhythm gingers the body to release adrenaline when working and listening to music. This substance is produced in the body when a person is excited, which makes the heart beat faster and increases one energy and ability to move quickly, thereby giving the person more strength to carry out a task. Some persons love to listen to music while studying; such individuals assimilate better, can accurately recall what they have read easily, and perform better at examinations.

Influence of Music in Insanity

A mental illness of such a severe nature that a person cannot distinguish fantasy from reality or conduct him or herself is referred to as insanity or madness. According to medical science, it is due to what is called psychosis, in other words, phobia or obsession of the mind. Causes of mental illness range from excessive abuse of drugs to extreme depression and spells. Research has proved listening to music may lessen the impact of obsession, depression and anxiety in a mentally insane person, irrespective of the cause of the insanity.

No matter how mentally insane a person is, in most cases, they respond to music; either they dance or become calm while listening to the rhythm. I have witnessed many mad persons dancing normally to music at different places and instances.

Influence of Music on Sporting Activity

Music contributes to energising physical body exercises. Exercises are enjoyed more when music is provided as a background. According to a study from the International Review for Sport and Exercise Psychology, self-selected motivational and suiting music enhances and improves energy ability, which leads to increased work output during repetitive endurance-type activities.

Influence of Music at the Start of the Day or Work

Between 1999 and 2000, I had a friend who worked in a marketing organisation that usually engages its staff in singing, clapping, and dancing every morning before going out to market its product. I later found out that this is to excite the workers emotionally and ginger their morals before going out to market their product. So far, the firm has marketed its product more effectively than any other at the time.

To achieve quick and effective results from your employees, especially in professions that involve direct labour for those who own businesses that manufacture or package products, make available some audio equipment where suiting music with a very strong rhythm is played in the background during their work time, this simple act or "un-seriousness" as some people might think it is; have the tendency to excite the workers and eliminate tensions, pressure and free their minds of the emotional problem as it motivates them to carry out their duty effectively and achieve better results.

In the Christian religion, serious believers usually start their day with what they call morning devotion. The devotion mainly includes singing, clapping, dancing, prayers, and sharing the holy Bible. This helps to make their day better and more effective. They become very free and tend to overcome the odds as they are excited to carry out their duties effectively for the day.

Starting your day with music goes a long way to easing emotional tension; music with a strong rhythm helps to release adrenaline and make you agile. When you wake up next, play mild and suitable music in the background as you prepare for work, preferably songs that you can sing along to and occasionally move the body to its rhythm.

Influence from Music Fraternities

Fraternity refers to a group of people sharing a common interest and mutual support based on a certain idea. Over the years, musicians have emerged with certain ideas that have influenced the lives of most youth.

Influences on youth include dressing, diction, lifestyle, and behaviours. In most cases, these influences are against certain moral or religious standards, but because the ideas are usually spread through music, the effect becomes very strong in the lives of both children and adults who are admirers.

For instance, in Nigeria and West Africa, a particular musician emerged with a style of music that at a time had influenced youth, and even children ages five and above were carried away by the rhythm of his music. His style of music is unique and danceable and comes with a particular dance, a step that is appealing to youth and also popular among some adults. His fans are ardent in his music and have adopted some of his lifestyle and ideas.

At a time, his admirers, who went by the name Malians, were suspected of having tried to promote the idea that education is not necessary; instead, acquiring a skill that brings in money daily to meet needs is the best and to an extent, a lot of youth were almost influenced by the professed idea.

A group of Pupils ages ten to fifteen were reportedly picked up during school hours by the police force from a primary school in southwest Nigeria because of the influence of Naira Marley's music; the set of children usually come to school with a turban on their head and are seen gathering at a particular place around the school and preferred to be addressed as Malians, this made certain individuals become uncomfortable and then invited the police. Although no particular crime or danger has been publicly reported in connection with the Malians, their appearance, i.e. dress pattern and lifestyle, possibly may cause some people to insinuate or suspect they might in the nearest future pose a threat to certain moral standards in society if their activities are not checked.

Similar groups or music fraternities that exist with a particular idea and belief that influence society in one way or another include the Rastafarians, who believe in the reverence of Jah and regard smoking weed as part of ritual activity in the worship of Jah. Most reggae musicians and lovers grow dreads, speak the patois or patua tone, and propagate Bob Marley's ideology as the front figure and performer of reggae and ska.

Hip hop, believed to have been registered as a religion, spreads its beliefs and objectives through music and has a great influence on the life of youth. One of the areas the hip-hop music fraternity has influenced society today is through their appearance, wearing expensive chains, sagging trousers, use of Vulgar words, and abuse of drugs, while some are involved in petty crimes.

Most of the provocative dressing and vulgar slang used by some of the youth today are influenced by the hip-hop music fraternity.

Some folks said, and I quote, "If we are to hope for a society of culturally literate people, music must be a vital part of our children."

(Credits to YO YO MA)

Soothing music brings great relief to the mind.

Chapter 5
The Dark Side of Music

Music has a dark side—when it is intertwined with diabolic forces to achieve harmful purposes. 'Diabolic' refers to evil practices intended to negatively influence the mind. The human mind is particularly vulnerable to such influences, as music has a profound connection with our emotions and cognitive processes.

The rhythm and melody of music are phenomenal and irresistible to humans, as there are usually certain responses that follow when we hear music. Music goes beyond the physical realm of entertainment; it has numerous spiritual interactions and connections to the spirit of man, and it is the only form of performing art that links the natural with the supernatural.

Wrong Assumption

A lot of you reading this book probably see music as the least expected means or medium that can be used against you diabolically, and that is why it is considered to be the most effective means by those in fetish practices against their victims.

Music easily connects with our inner being from which our mind can be controlled. There are cases where you come across a mentally insane person dancing without music being heard physically, but to their hearing, music is played. Another case is that of an individual who suddenly starts dancing without music being heard by those around; people who practice dark acts use music a lot to attack or control the minds of their victims to act to their bidding unknowingly.

The Use of Voodoo with Music

I have heard cases of a person who had initially refused to compromise to a decision but later changed his mind after listening to a piece of music targeted at him. I was once told a story about a particular folk musician in Lagos, Nigeria, who usually had a particular herb in his mouth while performing on stage, and once he started performing, people would empty their pockets and spray money on him as some usually come with a sac full of currencies and are all emptied on him.

There was an occasion when a man drove in on a newly acquired BMW to watch one of his musical performances; while performing, the musician mentioned his name, and the man stood up and danced to the rhythm of the music to the extent that he went and handed over to him the key of the car. The source who narrated this story to me told me that he watched the car owner trek while the musician drove past him with his newly gifted BMW.

The Use of Spells with Music

Spells are words that have magical powers to compel somebody to act in line with another person's influence. Spells are not myths. They exist and are used every day against victims unknowingly to them. Spells used with music are very effective because no one will ever suspect or detect if the lyrics of music that he or she is listening to are not just ordinary but spells because music is not in a solid or liquid form that one could easily detect that the texture or colour is abnormal.

There are a lot of music out there that are spells bound to accomplish a purpose in the life of people; musical spells are meant to influence the mind so that the person begins to act in a particular direction differently from whom or what he or she ought to be. Nowadays, All manner of music is being played without knowing which is which; we should be aware that certain attitudes displayed by some of the youth sometimes affect the music of the particular artist they often listen to.

The Use of Music with Mediumship

The practice of communicating with the dead and conjuring the spirits of the dead using certain powers through enchantment, incantations and songs is referred to as mediumship. Music plays a major role and is considered a frequency used to reconnect with spirit beings in such practices as necromancy and voodoo. So, special songs and musical instruments designed for such purposes are used to invoke and conjure different spirits.

Witch doctors make incantations with music to carry out their diabolic acts; African traditionalists use songs and special drums to attract or invoke the spirit of the ancestors in order to communicate with them. There are special drums, flutes, gongs, chimes and shakers used to carry out certain ritual practices across the world by those involved; all they need to do is play the particular musical instrument and make incantations through songs to achieve certain diabolism.

The Use of Music for Seduction

Music today has become the most effective tool for seduction. Seduction is defined as the act of persuading or displaying certain features or qualities to make something attractive with the aim of luring. Music is very effective when used as a seduction tool because of its connections with our minds and emotions. As a seductive, it penetrates through the mind easily and influences our actions gradually, then manifests physically. Most popular music genres today have vulgar lyrics; there is hardly popular music without words like touch, kiss, ass, boobs and several other dictions expressing romances and sex, which are the leading influence to rampant rape, underage sex and several forms of immoralities in our society today.

Youth are being seduced into alcoholism and drug abuse, such as smoking marijuana, opium, cocaine, heroin, etc., through music. Most musical videos shown on television usually display half-naked women with the male folks exploring their body parts, which in turn has an effect on the mind of the viewer in a way.

Words communicated with melody and rhythms are more effective and assimilative to the mind than those without. Children hardly forget lessons that are taught via songs but may hardly recall those taught with just words.

Music and Illuminati Scandal

The word Illuminati refers to a Bavarian secret society or cult founded on May 1st 1776, in Bavaria, today part of Germany; their major goal is to oppose religious influence over the society and the abuse of state power. The Illuminati believe they expose humanity to certain enlightenment they are ignorant of. In modern times, the Illuminati has imbibed every means possible to achieve their goals, and one of the most effective means is through the entertainment industry.

Most of our famous musicians and actors belong to the Illuminati cult. The members of the Illuminati are usually rich, have connections, and are celebrated globally. Musicians join the cult to trade their musical talents in return for popularity and wealth, which is why the Illuminati, in turn, use their music to influence the minds of the listeners to comply with their aims and objectives.

Allegedly, claim or fact, the Illuminati worship a god known as Baphomet, assumed to be the number eight on the scale below the ten generals of Satan. Illuminati members are believed to be associated with certain lifestyles that are contrary to moral and religious standards. Members of this cult are believed to be associated with a lifestyle such as excessive drive for sex, sodomy, abuse of drugs and profanity; their aim is to make sure teenagers and youth don't see the need to adhere to religious standards, to achieve that, they use music which is the fastest and most dominant means to get to the mind easily.

They find a suitable musician and inspire them to detect the lyrics, which are actually spells, so the artist could sing in styles and the language the people appreciate most to get their attention completely. They also inspire the beats and melodies of the music and detect how the artist will dress or appear to influence the minds of mostly youths.

That is why teenagers and youth are engaged in unlawful and uncontrolled sex practices, drug abuse and other petty crimes. Most youth today lack common decorum and moral values and no longer see the need to go to religious worship places any more, rather they prefer to gamble and get involved in gang activities as the level of exposure to immorality is alarming amongst teenagers because of the influence of certain music they love and always listing to; of course every good music is played on air it doesn't matter if it's a spell or not, but we do have choice on what genres and which musical artist to listen to.

The influence of spell-bound music is usually a gradual process as one keeps listening to it.

Children are the most defenceless entities in this case because their minds are gullible and eager to be fed with anything due to the fact that their neural paths are still tender and developing rapidly; in other words, bad music usually has a quick and more effect on children than adults.

It is improper to expose children to music with vulgar lyrics or musical videos showing sensitive parts of the body of male or female folks. I have watched a musical video that promotes marijuana; I have also seen a musical video promoting sex by showing all sorts of immoral displays; most times, these videos are not approved by the sensor board but are smuggled into the market one way or the other. I am not in any way condemning or promoting particular music; people have choices and reasons for liking particular music. It's all about what soothes you as the listener; I am only establishing that the type of music we love to listen to contributes a lot to our lifestyle as an individual.

*Music is so soothing that is never thought to
have a dark side.*

Chapter 6
Music as Therapy

Music therapy refers to the clinical use of music to accomplish specific individual goals, such as reducing stress and improving mood and self-expression. Conditions such as depression, substance abuse, Down syndrome, autism, Alzheimer's, dementia, and amnesia and, cardiac conditions, lower blood pressure, which usually affect a person's ability to function normally, are all brain-related and can be improved using music therapy.

The therapy simply involves listening to music, singing, playing an instrument and composing music.

Music therapy helps psychologically, emotionally, physically, spiritually, cognitively, and socially. Research has shown that listening to soothing music can reduce anxiety, blood pressure, and pain and improve sleep quality, mood, mental alertness, and memory, as these are all brain-oriented conditions.

Exposure to musical activities for children before birth and continued after birth from an early age helps to block any chance of brain disorder because music increases brain plasticity, changing neural pathways by enabling the perfect level of adaptability.

Music Therapy in Baby Blues

After having a baby, many women, especially young mothers experiencing childbirth for the first time, may feel sad, worried, or tired in the days following delivery. This experience is what is referred to as baby blues or postpartum depression. Music therapy sessions for pregnant women during antenatal care contribute to improved well-being and decreased symptoms of postpartum depression, particularly for young mothers.

An experiment was conducted, babies before they could walk and talk, were given musical lessons such as singing nursery rhymes accompanied by musical instruments; babies who had the lessons communicated better, smiled more, related easily and showed earlier and more superior brain responses to not just music alone but other activities.

Science research has proven that babies recognize a theme from a television show or advert before birth, as well as the music their mother usually hears. Babies who are exposed to music before birth through their mother usually have their brains develop quickly and display intellectual abilities soon after birth.

Studies have also shown babies can detect the differences in musical tone and changes in the tempo (speed) and the rhythm (the style of beat) of music. They are also able to know when a melody changes to a different key (tone). Babies as young as two months show preference, i.e. choice for a consonant musical sound (harmony) over a discordant sound.

According to a study conducted at Belfast University, babies two weeks before birth recognize the difference between the theme of music and a popular TV show heard daily by their mothers; this further proves how profound and effective music can be in children's lives.

Reducing the Rate of Mental Disorder Using Music Therapy

Brain-related challenges such as autism and Down syndrome are always associated with very low IQ and are common with mostly children and usually occur at an early age, and they grow up with it to become adults.

The signs are usually noticed at six months of age when the child is not active and responding to certain stimuli as expected of his or her age. Early exposures to music, such as suiting songs or melodies, restrict the risk of a child having any of these brain disorders. Pregnant mothers at a stage, most especially when the baby's movement is beginning to be felt, should create time to listen to suitable music and sometimes sing rhymes while rubbing the belly. Classical music is fantastic in achieving such a purpose; music composed by Wolfgang Amadeus Mozart has been recommended to help the brain develop quickly.

Music Therapy as Preventive Measures

Children from infants to one year should constantly be sung to or made to listen to mild music (Lullaby). Children aged **two** should be taught simple nursery rhymes and melodies and also provided with toy musical instruments for fun.

Children aged three and four can learn to sing and play percussive musical objects such as the glockenspiel, xylophone bells and handheld percussions. Children aged five can learn to play the recorder and the keyboard and be introduced to simple melodies and rhythms. Children aged seven and above can learn to sight-read music, sing songs and play certain musical instruments they can physically handle themselves.

Music Therapy for Brain Ailment

The use of music as rehabilitation has proven very effective in helping persons with brain-related ailments improve.

Autism and Down syndrome are as a result of certain cells in the brain that are responsible for communicating certain actions or functions becoming inactive; the solution therefore is to reactivate those cells so they can start to interact properly with other cells that carry information to other part of the body so the individual can start doing what he or she is unable to do before now.

Children or adults with autism or Down syndrome should be engaged in special music training by a music specialist, not just a musician or music teacher; a music specialist is one with the skills to teach music to rehabilitate a person.

Musical activity has been proven to be the most effective means of activating and strengthening brain cells because, as a stimulus, music is usually processed by receptors for sensing and reacting to it especially; as this is done, the neural connection within the two cerebral hemispheres and other neurons that carries information to various part of the body become more active and as a result propels the body motor to act, at this point the individual start by attempting to do things he could not do before now, in the process of time as the music rehabilitation continues, the individual improves drastically.

Music therapy involves logic and ethics, as well as lots of patience and a period of time, depending on the level of the disorder. For parents whose child has a brain condition, it is wise to include musical activity alongside the medications because neuroscience studies have proven that music can provoke certain chemicals in the brain, which helps to improve brain activity, thereby restoring damage.

Those who are incapacitated and might not be able to help themselves can employ the services of a musician who can play the guitar or the piano and sing. The musician can sing for the patient, and over time, the patient will start to respond by attempting to sing along, which becomes his or her beginning point for improvement.

Music is an effective tool for improving and healing brain damage.

Chapter 7
Knowing the Music That Is Best for You

Just as there are preferences in what we eat, how we dress and go about things, also it is with music. People have a choice in terms of the style and pattern of music they want to hear at a time or all the time. There is a popular saying that a man's meat is another's poison, so it is with music. People prefer particular music genres and patterns that soothe their hearing. Genre, in this context, refers to a major class or category of music.

Music Preference

In history, music is grouped into three major styles or genres: folk, classical, and pop. Each genre or style houses several patterns and is either secular or religious by objectives. Religious music is either Islamic, Gospel, Hindu, etc.

Some people prefer music based on religion or other personal objectives. An individual might prefer pop genres, but only a particular pattern of pop might appeal to him or her. Others might prefer classical music, but maybe the symphony is their preferred pattern.

The pattern in music refers to the different ways in which a particular person decides to play a genre of music to sound unique from the main style. For example, reggae is associated with Jamaican folk music, but today, it has different patterns, such as western reggae, root reggae, and island reggae. An individual might love reggae music, but only the island reggae pattern most appeals to him or her. Another might also love classical music genres, but the concert orchestra is probably the preferred pattern for him or her.

The Music That Yields Positive Results

A lot has been said regarding the effects and benefits of music in previous chapters, but the fact is that it is only when music soothes the listener that it can be absolved into the listener's mind and then bring about the positive effects and benefits.

Some people only listen to music with a religious objective because of certain strictures. We also have those who don't mind; they just like to listen to music irrespective of genres, patterns, or objectives, but once it is music, they are good to go.

But it is important to note that music to the mind is like the food we eat; when we eat junk, we become prone to certain ailments, but when we eat cautiously, we tend to stay healthy. Music is good generally, but not all music is appropriate at a time; some might be best at certain events, and some might not; certain music may not be appropriate for certain gatherings.

Music has the best positive effect when it is heard appropriately. For example, when an individual is stressed out, music with a very strong rhythm might not really be appropriate to help refresh the mind; rather, calming and soothing music will be needed at the time.

Music and Our Age

Our age at a given point in life determines our choice of the type of music we like to listen to. What attracts a child might just be what an adult sees and passes over without giving it a second look.

At one time, we might like the fast tempo of rock music and the steady beat of ska, but as time went by, we might suddenly see that we can no longer break dance or do reggae skank. Certain music may not really appeal to us anymore at certain ages; at some stage, we might prefer the gentle rhythm of soul, high life, or the blues to the stomps of hip-hop music.

As children, we love the shallow sounds of the harpsichord and the twinkling of the chimes in lullabies, but to a certain age, the music becomes childish to our hearing. Our elderly folks in the village or countryside might not really appreciate the hip hop or the dance hall except for a few who might just want to give audience to the music but might not really take it to heart; also, you don't expect the youth mostly in urban development to appreciate a traditional folk music style or an orchestra piece except for very few. To some extent, our age at a time can bring about caution towards listening to certain music that may no longer be appropriate for us.

Listening to Music with a Target

Listening to music having a target at heart is Synonymous to applying the doctor's prescription for particular ailment. A patient must adhere to the doctor's prescription to get well.

It is vital to listen to music with a target or purpose in mind in order for you to enjoy its benefits; you can play and listen to music with the aim to relax the mind, cheer the heart, free you from certain burdens at heart, celebrate, free muscles through dance, or boost excitement.

When you are able to get the music that soothes your needs at a time, and you play and listen to it, your mind will easily absolve the lyrics, the rhythm and the melody, which will, in return, bring about the result that is needed. Although popular music genres are assumed to have melodies and rhythm that appeal to a wider audience, not everyone prefers pop in leisure time. Classical music is effective in helping persons with certain brain conditions to improve; music with a strong rhythm triggers adrenaline to promote good body movement.

Calm music helps to inspire the mind if you are involved in a creative career, and if you need some excitement, pop genres with very strong rhythms can do the job perfectly. You should know the music that meets your various emotional, intellectual, health, and mental needs at a time and use it appropriately.

For religious-minded individuals, there is lots of religious music that promotes your belief either as a Muslim, Christian, Jew, Hindi, etc.; it is advisable to listen to them when you need an uplift in the spirit or for enlightenment. For the free thinker, there is also music that promotes your ideas; listen to them. For people involved in traditional practices, traditional music is the best to help you achieve the objectives. Pop music will provide all the entertainment and grooves needed for social events and purposes. Music is unsuitable for children at a particular age; parents or guardians need some discretion when listening to certain music with the children present.

Certain music is not to be heard by children below eighteen years because of some lyrical content that might not be suitable; some music has lyrics that are not ideal for children because some music is basically meant to promote romance and should only be heard by mature adults.

Words spoken through music tend to replay in our consciousness because of the melody rather than just words spoken without melodies. Music should be heard on target for positive effects and benefits; when you feel low, listen to music that can cheer you up.

Music heard at the right moment provides great relief to the mind.

Chapter 8
Acquiring a Skills in Music

Skills mean ability; a skill in music refers to an ability to play a musical instrument, sight reading scores, compose songs and ear training through sol-fa notations. The intellectual, health and emotional benefits we get from listening and enjoying the rhythm and melody of music can't be compared with the numerous intellectual benefits it has on those who play instruments, sing or can read musical scores.

According to neurosciences, playing an instrument, composing, singing or reading music increases one's ability to pay attention to happenings in the environment, make decisions, process language, solve problems and have a better memory. The benefit of acquiring a skill in music is the following:

1. Enhances Neural Communication,
It helps the combination of electrical and chemical signals on both sides of the brain to keep it functioning and become stronger, improving an individual's learning skills and memory. A person who plays a musical instrument or instruments is very creative, calculates, reasons, and usually comes up with better ideas than those without the skill.

2. Promote Fine Motor Skill,
This means that the functions that involve specific movements of the body muscles in performing certain tasks in the individual become more efficient, including verbal and nonverbal reasoning. It makes your movement perfect, and you become more careful and calculative when walking, driving, drawing, or doing anything that has to do with the use of your body part.

Acquiring skills in music is not just for fun, but because of the neurological effects it has. Some adults think acquiring skills in music is only meant for children and the youth, while others consider it irrelevant for persons who are way past a particular age. In some developed countries, special musical classes are organized for the elderly to help curtail certain ailments that are linked to the brain at a certain age.

My Personal Experience

The use of musical activities to improve the condition of persons with low I.Q. has proven to be very effective. At a time, I was working with a school as a music specialist and had a case of a student with low I.Q due to an accident that occurred two days after their birth as twins. He had difficulties learning and recalling things he had been taught. Although other medical measures were not completely effective, the first day he attended the musical class, out of all the musical instruments available, he showed interest in learning the jazz drum kits. At first, I was like, woo, why the jazz drum kit? It would not be an easy task considering his condition, but anyway, I decided to take the bull by the horns, and I never knew that would help improve his condition fast.

So, I started by introducing him to the rudiments of jazz drum. Many of you may not really know how complex playing the jazz drum kit is; someone might just say, "What is complicated about the drum kits? After all, is it not to sit and start hitting the percussions?" You are right, but there is something complicated about playing the jazz drum kits that you are about to learn right now. First, you don't just sit and hit the drum kits; you must ensure everything rhymes to make meaning to the ears. First, let me expose you to the technicalities involved in playing the jazz drum.

The jazz drum refers to the modern drum that consists of an average of eight percussions. Some have sixteenth to thirty-two, and the advanced type has sixty-four kits or percussions and has to be played by just one person at a time. However, the standard type that is common has eight to ten percussions.

In playing the drum kits, the bass drum and the hi-hats are the major percussions that provides the rhythmic background that every other percussion follows thereafter, but the problem is; each of these percussions plays something different from each other at the same time and has to rhyme.

The right foot pedals the bass drum differently from what the right hand plays on the hi-hat; simultaneously, the left hand plays something differently on the snare drum. Why does the left foot also control the hi-hat on its pedal differently, so the two hands and the two feet all play different rhythms that must all rhyme together to make meaning to the ears?

At this point, the brain is divided to carry out four different tasks at a time, and the player must concentrate and coordinate to make sure all he or she plays using the two hands and both feet blend to make meaning to the listener so at this point the brain is multi-tasked. By engaging the brain this way, it activates the action potentials in the left and right cerebral hemispheres, which in turn also affect every other nerve or neuron that communicates certain actions to the rest part of our body by strengthening them to become more active and effective.

Back to my experience, I had no choice but to start teaching him to play the drum kits; his IQ was low to the extent that a few minutes after I showed him how to sit on the drum stool, he couldn't remember again, that was very strange isn't it? But I kept on applying the techniques in teaching music as therapy; within a period of time, he was able to play the bass drum and the hi-hat together; from that point, you know that a part of his brain that wasn't functioning accurately before now has started to function, the nerves that involve specific movement of the body muscles in performing certain task in the brain are now reactivated, from that point he picked up, the action potential in him and his intelligence quotients increased and it affected his academics performances.

His class teacher called my attention to his improvement, as at the time this book was written, he should have rounded up the university.

A year later, the school had another student who couldn't speak clearly, couldn't feed himself, or couldn't coordinate himself at age eight.

His I.Q. was so low that he needed to be supervised and assisted when copying notes. Otherwise, he could spend hours copying just a few lines of the note and not be able to copy them correctly.

During breakfast and lunch, the teacher on duty will have to wait for an extra thirty minutes for him to finish his meal. He became another special student I had; the first day I attended the music class, he picked interest in blowing the Recorder, a woodwind musical instrument which is not that really as complicated as the drum or the keyboard. When we started, at first, holding the recorder and covering the holes was a difficult task, but gradually, he began to pick up and later got the logic, and in the process of time, he could play some of the nursery rhymes and became one of the top in the team.

His IQ increased at an alarming rate, and before I resigned from the organization, he could speak better, become smarter, feed himself, and copy his notes fast and correctly. I can go on and on about how effective musical skills have improved people's intelligence and social skills, but let's continue with other points.

Physical Conditions for Acquiring Musical Skills
Obtaining a skill in music may be limited, provided the individual is breathing and can hear. A condition that may not allow a person to learn a skill in music is being deaf and dumb or, worse, dead and buried.

But it's amazing to know that a man called Ludwig Beethoven, 1770-1829, one of the world's celebrated Romantic music composers, defied his deafness at a time in his life to continue to compose classical pieces. In fact, some of his best compositions came later in his life when he was partially deaf.

I have had students I taught in a school of music who were completely blind; the first learnt how to play the jazz drum, and the other came after the first learnt how to play the keyboard. I discovered they learnt faster compared to those who could see. A person who is dumb but hears can acquire a skill in music as an instrumentalist on any musical instrument of choice. A person who is completely paralyzed but can hear and talk can learn to sing; an individual in a wheelchair can learn to play every other musical instrument except for the drum kits. The only restriction to acquiring a skill in music is if a person is deaf or dumb.

Age Limit in Acquiring a Skill in Music

We can all learn a skill in music regardless of our age. Children aged one to three can be taught to sing rhymes and play toy musical instruments for fun. The optimal age for children to learn and play standard musical instruments is five.

Manufacturers of musical instruments have standard mini and medium-size instruments, such as drum kits, saxophones, trumpets, Guitars, and violins, for children of various ages to be able to handle and learn to play.

There is no age limit to acquiring musical skills. All that matters is interest. I had a coursemate when I was in the school of music who enrolled upon learning that she was three months pregnant and was learning to play the trumpet. It startled people, and a doctor was consulted to understand the implications, but the doctor said it was all right for her to continue. Now I know what positive effect that will have on the baby inside her and after birth.

Acquiring a skill in music at an early age will make the child intellectually and socially polished, and will also help to restrain certain brain-related ailments that affect the child's intelligence. Learning music at an advanced or even old age is wonderful as it will keep the brain active and functioning at its best and also increases the chances of longevity by containing the negative effects of certain health challenges associated with old age and making the person live a little longer. An individual at a hundred years old can still acquire a skill in music if they have the strength to press the keyboard keys or pluck the strings of the guitar and, most importantly, the interest at heart.

Musical Skills You Can Acquire at Certain Age

The fact has been established that skills in music can be acquired irrespective of age, sex, religion, and for certain health challenges, except for the deaf and the dumb. But the truth is that we can be limited by age to learning certain musical instruments; for example, a child of one to three years old cannot be able to handle the saxophone or the trumpet and blow it due to the size and weight, so he or she has to learn a musical instrument that they can handle. There is no doubt some children have special abilities (prodigy). In such cases, they shouldn't be limited. Wolfgang Amadeus Mozart 1732-1809, when he was four years old, could learn a piece of music in thirty minutes; at age five, he could play a keyboard musical instrument called the Clavier so well that people could hardly believe that a child of his age could play that way, at the age of six he was composing the largest piece of classical music known as the symphony. When he turned eight years old,

Wolfgang Amadeus Mozart constantly travelled around Europe with his father, who also played the violin.

His composition is today found to be effective in improving persons with low IQ and other brain-related ailments even after hundreds of years of his demise. A person at an advanced age is not expected to start learning to play the jazz drum kits since he did not start early, but sometimes interest and determination should not be underestimated, aside; the body of a sixty-year-old or above might not have that much physical strength needed to play the drum kit. Everybody must not learn to play an instrument; you could learn to sing or to sight read music scores and do it privately.

Musical Skills as Mental Exercise

Our brain also functions like the battery we use in our mobile phones or cars; although much more powerful, it can run down and shut us off temporarily or permanently. People go on commas when their brain is temporarily shut down or, in the worst cases, they become brain dead, although alive but functionless. In several cases, when all efforts have been made to revive the person, and all seem to no avail, the doctors will advise that they are better to let go.

At that time, I had a Samsung tablet with a cracked screen, which affected its touch functionality but still powered on. I did not need it immediately, so I only bothered to charge it once it completely shut down. The tablet wouldn't turn on when I finally needed it, even after charging it for several hours. I took it to a technician who informed me that the battery was damaged because it hadn't been charged for an extended period and needed to be replaced. Like a device, our brains also need regular mental exercises to stay active and effective.

Neuroscience has proved musical skills to be a fantastic mental exercise; as mental exercise skills in music help the brain to achieve elasticity, in other words, to become more flexible or expandable to enable it to contain any input hundred per cent, like when you upgrade the gigabyte on your computer to enable it to carry more storage without having to drag and become slow in accessing or processing information. When we actively engage our brain with musical activities such as singing, playing musical instruments, and sight reading music scores, our brains become more effective and function at full capacity without limitations.

A skill in music is essential for balancing your nature.

Chapter 9
Effects of Specific Musical Instruments on the Brain

Musical instruments are designed differently and also require different techniques to play. In terms of listening to music, there are no special skills needed, but to play any musical instrument, much study is required. Learning to play musical instruments has nothing to do with an individual having the talent; instead, it requires determination, discipline and concentration to achieve because the process teaches self-control, perseverance, diligence and teamwork.

The brain's response to learning musical instruments varies based on the specific techniques required for producing rhythm, melodies, and harmony. For example, the logic required to play the trumpet is more complex compared to that of a saxophone. The trumpet has just three valves, which you manipulate to produce all the pitches and keys in music, but the saxophone has several levers you manipulate to achieve them easily.

When learning to play the trumpet, the brain responds differently than when learning to play the saxophone. Each musical instrument contributes to improving brain function uniquely. Let's look at the various ways each of these three basic musical instruments—keyboard, rhythm Guitar, and jazz drum set—including the art of singing—improves our brain functions.

Playing the Jazz Drum

Jazz drums refer to a set of seven to eight percussions connected to each other and played by one person. Both hands and feet are involved when playing the jazz drum, as the player synchronizes all four limbs to work together simultaneously, requiring the use of both sides of the brain simultaneously. An activity of this nature increases an individual's IQ level.

Neuroscience research has proven that playing the drum kits propels the brain to release a substance called endorphins, which create feelings of happiness, pleasure and excitement; endorphins are also the body's own morphine-like pain killer, which helps control pains and those suffering grief. Drumming induces deep relaxation, lowers blood pressure and reduces stress. Drumming and rhythm are powerful tools as they saturate the entire brain, boosting the player's academic performance, especially in math; drummers play according to timing.

Playing the Rhythm Guitar

A musical instrument with strings stretched from one point to another that the player plucks and frets to make music is called a guitar. The guitar is either the bass guitar or the rhythm guitar, which has four strings and produces the lowest tone among other instruments.

The rhythm guitar has six strings and mostly plays chord progression in music, such as picks, vamp, strum, or solo. Playing the guitar promotes focus, discipline and patience because

The players usually combine the strings, picking them using specific fingers at a particular point to form harmony and producing a certain pitch needed to progress to songs.

The process at the beginning is painful as it usually causes strains and lumps on the tip of the fingers, but with the determination of the players to continue, it automatically improves one's coordination and finger Motor skills. Research also has shown that playing the guitar improves memory and cognitive skills.

The rhythmic strumming or finger-picking techniques used in guitar play create a soothing and meditating experience, promoting relaxation and reducing the stress hormone cortisol. People who can play the guitar possess unique cognitive, emotional, and social skills that contribute to their character and intelligence. The ability to play the guitar stimulates various areas of the brain, enhancing memory, problem-solving ability, emotional intelligence and coordination.

Playing the Keyboard

Musical instruments that have keys arranged in a row, mostly white and black, that the player uses fingers to press to make music are called keyboards. Examples include the piano, the organ, the harpsichord, and the synthesizer. Because of the techniques involved in playing, keyboard musical instruments appear to be particularly beneficial to the brain.

Like the drum set, playing the keyboard requires both hands, but each finger on both hands is coordinated and controlled in a unique way to produce a simultaneous touch referred to as the arpeggios, including the two cerebral hemispheres, to progress to the song.

Studies show that learning to play the keyboard can be very helpful in improving brain function and is an effective way to enhance the structure of what is referred to as white matter in neurosciences. White matter refers to the configuration of the brain that plays a critical role in helping the body process information. It connects areas that send and receive signals, affecting the ability to focus and learn, solve problems, and stay balanced when walking. Playing the keyboard improves verbal memory, particularly, and also builds good habits, focus, perseverance, diligence, and creativity.

As an adult, it helps to experience decreased depression, fatigue, and anxiety as well as improve memory, verbal communication and sense of independence.

Singing

The art of using the voice in expression with melody and rhythm is called singing, or, in simple words, the use of voice to make music. The fact is that everyone can sing, and the interesting thing is that you don't have to be a good singer before enjoying the effects and benefits it brings to the brain. Once you can put one or two words together with melody and rhythm, you can feel the impact right in you.

Singing is good for everyone at all levels as it lowers stress, boosts immunity, and improves lung function. It also enhances memory by helping you store information or things you have learnt and recall them even without having to look into a book.

The ability to sing improves mental health and helps you cope with physical and emotional pain. When singing a soothing song, your brain is flooded with a substance called dopamine, a type of chemical in the brain that gives a feeling of pleasure, satisfaction, and motivation.

Singing, instrumentation, and dance are genuine conduits of dopamine in the body. Among other things, the dopamine that our brain gets flooded with as a result of singing is a lot more wholesome than the dopamine we get from notifications on our phones.

Also, when singing songs with a strong rhythm, our brain releases dopamine, which in turn releases another substance called endorphins; endorphins are another brain chemical that alleviates pain, lowers stress, improves mood, enhances our well-being, and causes us to get naturally high when singing in a group.

The ability to play a specific musical instrument can provide the satisfaction the mind needs to achieve stability.

Chapter 10
Advantages of Learning Musical Instruments

Learning to play a musical instrument increases flexibility to any age-related decline in hearing and keeps the brain sharp. Scientific research and studies prove that the ability to play a musical instrument fuels the brain in a very powerful way because music is connected with our emotions.

Brain scans have been able to identify the difference in the brain pattern of a serious musician and a non-musician. The huge bundle of tiny wire-like tissues called nerve fibres that connect the two sides of the brain in a person who learns or can play a musical instrument or instruments is found to be larger compared to those who don't have such skills.

The advantage of this is that such people have better listening ability, can understand quickly how things work technically, reason fast, and have better body coordination, most especially for those who play the keyboard and the jazz drum.

The ability to play a musical instrument changes the brain structure and, as a result, causes the brain to function better by improving long-term memory and leading to better brain development. Those who started at a young age are of better advantage; according to research from the University of Montreal, people who play musical instruments tend to be more mentally alert, accurate and quick to acquire, retain and recall memories.

There are great advantages when a person starts to learn musical instruments at an early age; learning musical instruments at an early age causes the most radical changes in the brain, and even a brief period of instrumental training can have long-lasting benefits on children. Generally, learning to play musical instruments increases greyish nervous tissues, controls cell bodies and fibres in various brain regions and strengthens the connection between the cerebral hemispheres.

According to neuroscience discoveries, the ability to play musical instruments enhances verbal memory, spatial reasoning, and literacy skills, especially in children.

A study conducted in 2013 by scientists worldwide also proves that the skill of playing musical instruments helps speech processing and learning in children with impaired ability. That means children who can play musical instruments read better and understand more easily than their counterparts.

I will encourage everyone to learn particular musical instruments. If possible, it should be made compulsory for children due to the lasting effect it usually has on their brains at an early age.

Several scientific research studies have proved that learning musical instruments can help improve the brain in several ways, most especially for children. Learning a skill in music early protects the brain against ailments such as dyslexia, dementia and Down syndrome and to

- Strengthen bond
- Strengthen memory and reading skills
- Makes them happy
- Help them process multiple things at a time
- Increase blood flow in the brain
- Helps the brain to recover from certain damages
- Reduces stress and depression
- Strengthen the brain's executive function drastically

It has also been found that children who undergo a year and four-month musical training display more powerful structural and functional brain changes.

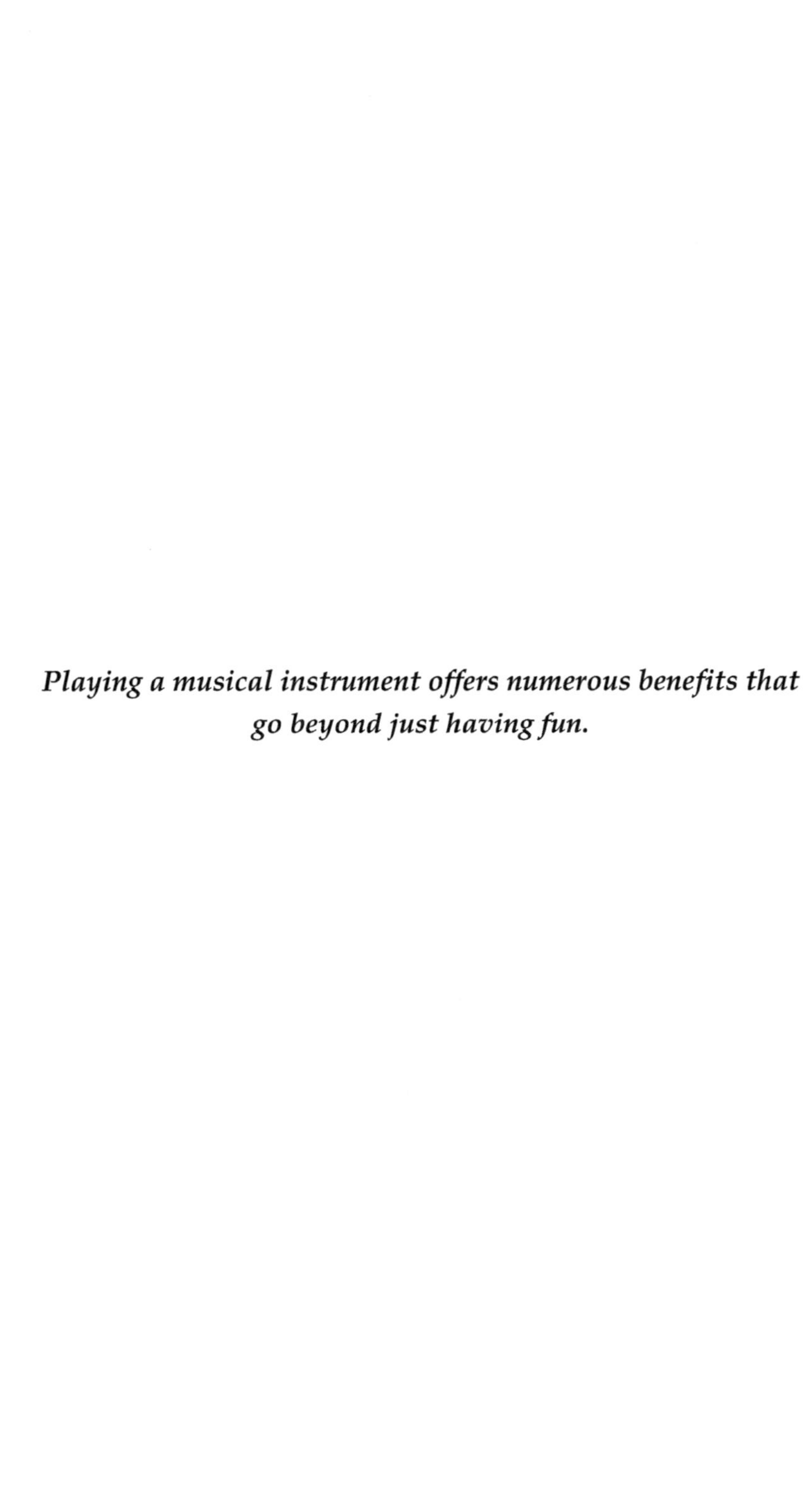

Playing a musical instrument offers numerous benefits that go beyond just having fun.

Chapter 11

Music in School Curriculum

Many schools do not offer music as part of the subject; some do due to the expenses that the subject incurs, considering the cost of musical instruments needed and their maintenance, including the teacher's salary. Very few schools offer music as a subject on its own; the majority offer it under cultural and creative art, which does not allow the subject to be taken so that the needed knowledge, skill and intellectual benefits are achieved.

One of the only activities that activate, stimulate and use the entire brain at a time is music; musical activities such as singing, sight reading score and the ability to play a musical instrument are beneficial as they improve our ability in manual and physical skills referred to as psychomotor in a technical term, musical knowledge also affects our mental skills and area of knowledge (cognitive) and as well as our attitude and self-discipline (Affective). In most schools, music as a subject in school is considered unnecessary, and sometimes religious sentiments are brought into it; this is the reason why the level of intelligence in children and youth, including adults in such places, mostly in some underdeveloped nations, is very low and backwards because where there are intellectuals, inventions and innovations which brings about development is inevitable. Music offered as a subject in school shouldn't be regarded as a second-class subject or an extracurricular activity that is less important compared to the other subjects. Music is a central part and essential to an all-inclusive and important school. Music is the only subject that has the ability to affect knowledge of every other subject. There is the mathematical aspect of music in the calculation of beat and measures referred to as time signature; there is the chemistry aspect of music in the formation of chords and various conditions by which the chords are applied in a progression using formulas; there is the physics aspect of music in the study of how sounds are synchronized to produce several textures, there is the biological aspect of music in the aspect of manipulating the voice for optimum output in connection with the lungs, there is the history aspect of music which exposes you to several musical events in the past and times and seasons of particular style or genres, there is the social aspect, the linguistic aspect, the geographical aspect etc. music is broad and covers a wide range of knowledge.

The Origin of Music as Part of Learning in Schools

The Greeks were the first to introduce music as part of the subject taken in schools because of the intellectual and emotional benefits. In AD 500, the Greeks already had an organized form of their folk music and had made musical lessons compulsory in their schools. They also established independent musical schools where persons who missed the opportunity at an early age could enrol to acquire the skills. No doubt, Greek philosophers such as Pythagoras experimented with musical scales to achieve certain mathematical results to invent.

The Greeks became the influence of Western civilization, which is still enjoyed today; knowledge, invention and great philosophers emerged from all over Greek city-states; the secret lies in their intellectual abilities, which in no doubt was a result of their exposure to musical abilities.

The most organized form or style of music (The orchestra) started with the Greeks.

Orchestra music is complicated at all levels and requires serious thinking in a logical way to compose and perform; this has proven to be why most ancient Greeks were intellectuals who thought reason logically. Most parents think music taught in schools or taken as extra lessons is a waste of time or a distraction to a child's academics; rather, musical skills help a child to reason logically and assimilate better what he or she is taught. Music has a deep effect, most especially on children, because their minds are still developing at a speedy rate and are easily influenced.

The following are reasons why you should enrol your child in a school that offers music as part of learning. Musical lessons help the child to develop language and reasoning skills. The area of the brain related to language and reasoning is the left side, which usually develops better with music, and by this, the child can learn fast and recall easily what he or she has been taught. The ability to constantly perform a piece of music by sight or heart can save students well in education. Musical ability helps promote the skill of making things in the area of creativity, coming out with masterpieces instead of second-rate.

Students learning to play musical instruments or who can play musical instruments have better hand-eye coordination and movement.

Other benefits of teaching music as part of a child's school curriculum include:

- A sense of achievement.
- Success in society.
- Emotional development.
- Exposure to a wide range of things.

Schools that teach music as a compulsory subject to their pupils usually produce graduating students who are creative and exhibit certain qualities compared to their counterparts or schools whose music is not included in their lessons.

A school, by its purpose, shouldn't be only where a child goes to learn math, science, etc., alone, but also to have his or her character moulded, including their social quotients developed and built for the future. Therefore, social activities such as singing, instrumental music, and dance, which are comprised of music and are undoubtedly an inevitable activity in humanity, should also be allowed as part of the school curriculum.

Whether we accept it or not, music has become a great influence in the lives of mostly the youth and children; they are more current in musical trends than their parents; one way or the other, they are exposed to music. Music is part of humanity and, in some cases, more patronized than other forms of art. The simple act of making music naturally brings about the following important qualities in students,

Self-Regulation

A sense or the ability to act in a way considering the long-term consequence of what an action today might bring tomorrow.

Self Confidence

They have a positive attitude towards what they can do at the time and trust in them to do it without fear of failure.

Leadership Skill

An ability to take and maintain decisive measures to plan and to bring about achieving set goals.

Social Skills

The ability to communicate, interact, mix up or associate with others to help or to get help others to get along with others, make friends, develop healthy relationships, etc.

Social Emotional Intelligence

The ability to be aware of one's feelings in the present moment, interact with people, work as a team, learn from others to socialize. We can't deny that music is a major influence among youth and society as our children are confronted with such reality. The proper perspective of art needs to be part of their learning in school to guide them properly in the art for those who might want to pursue music as a career.

Music is a wonderful gift to humanity, though it has yet to be fully embraced by many.

Chapter 12
The Concluding Part

Today, music has become one of the fastest ways to influence society. Children aged ten and above are often more familiar with trending songs and dances than most adults. Various types of music are played everywhere—in the streets, on the radio, and in public places—with little to no restrictions in most areas. The uses of music are versatile, ranging from skits on social media to street performances and sales of products in marketplaces. Nowadays, you hear children sing songs you don't even know, and they can even tell you the name of the artist and the trends in them. Personally, I got to know about Burner

Boy for the first time in early 2021 through my students who are between the ages of 8 – 10; when I asked them to list some of the artists they know, they mentioned the name and some of the song he sang, before then I was yet to hear about Mr Burner, despite he is a Nigerian and he was in Nigeria and I am a Nigerian and in Nigeria too.

Whether we like it or not, our children and youth are already engrossed with trending music and various dances that accompany them. Music is a major influence in society, either negative or positive, and will continue to be so long as life continues. Music can influence the mind and program it towards a particular direction; we should be aware that good music for our mind is medicine for emotional ailments. Music goes beyond just being entertainment; it heals the mind and can also harm the mind depending on the contents; it is a wonderful gift to humanity that has never been noticed by so many; music has contributed a whole lot to our daily lives and activities.

Music should be heard with discretion, and the lyrics should be considered. Not all music is meant for us, especially children, because negative or positive Ideas and certain influences are easily passed on through music. Children's porous and tender minds easily adapt to songs and melodies, which can influence them for a very long time.

The essentials of music must be taught in schools. Children should be guided about music, and parents should caution their children about the kinds of songs they listen to. Even as adults, philosophies and ideologies communicated using music are more effective, stick easily, and have a lasting effect on the mind than those communicated just with words.

Music on its own is never intended to harm as it is meant to heal the spirit mind, but when used negatively or combined with fetish practices or spells, music becomes harmful to the mind.

Musical Career

Music careers are lucrative; musicians today charge up to a million dollars and more to perform just for a few hours. Popular musicians also promote products for companies and are paid handsomely. Some musicians are even more popular than the political elites as they have more admirers in society.

Parents whose children display certain musical talents should find a way of helping them develop the skill rather than discouraging them. Most parents detest their children's pursuit of a music career, but the irony is that many of these parents who won't let their children pursue a career in music would pay millions to invite a musician who is another person whose child was allowed by his or her parent to pursue the career to come and entertain them during special events and other ceremonies.

A lot of parents consider music to be a distraction to their children's academics; parent will ask their children to suspend musical activities because of an exam; little did they know that music connects together the two halves of the brain at a time, which makes the brain more powerful and absorbs as much as many information and lessons that are passed unto the person and same time helps the person to recall what he or she has learnt accurately.

Pursuing a Career in Music

Music, like every other career, can be studied in higher institutions and in private schools of music; the requirements to study music are just basic literacy or numeracy. An individual going into the career should first acquire knowledge of music rudiments alongside the skills in singing and playing a musical instrument. Music careers are divided into two aspects: musicianship and choreography. Musicianship deals with the aspect of vocals and instrumentation, and choreography deals with the uses of the body in response to music.

A person doesn't need to be talented to pursue a career in music; all that is needed is the desire and the passion, and you do not need to have a good voice to become a singer because there are provisions to be trained to have a good voice. All that is needed to play musical instruments is an individual ability to use his mouth, hands and legs. All a vocalist needs is his or her mouth; a drummer needs both hands and legs; some musical instruments require only the mouth, and some only fingers are required.

I am only writing just a little about what music does to us as humans. Aside from neuron sciences, music also has numerous spiritual benefits for those of us who belong to one religion or the other. To me, music is divine and has marvellous connections to the things of the mind in a way beyond physical reasoning.

Take advantage of music by creating time, especially to listen to music that suits you. Afford yourself a particular skill in music that you can use to keep yourself busy in place of anxiety and as a way to avoid certain disturbances.

Persons with musical abilities have several health advantages over those without the skills. In summary, identify the style of music that best soothes your hearing, create time to listen to your desired music, and engage in musical activity of your choice. Music, as simple as it is, is a powerful phenomenon and one of God's greatest gifts to humanity; explore it and use it maximally.

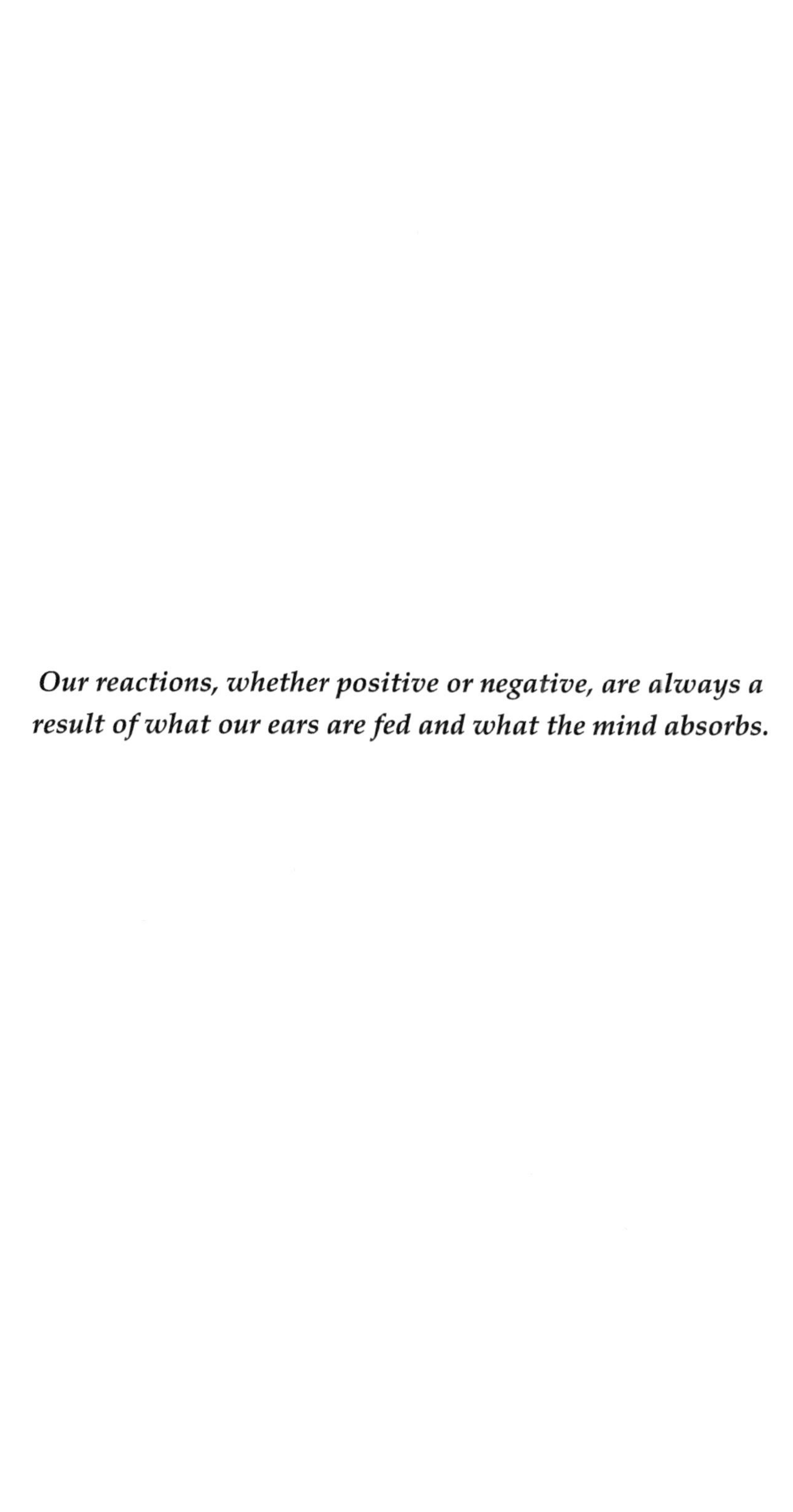

Our reactions, whether positive or negative, are always a result of what our ears are fed and what the mind absorbs.

9 788119 524983